SHIRE GARDEN HISTORY

The English Landscape Garden

MILES HADFIELD

Published in 1997 by Shire Publications Ltd, Cromwell House, Church Street, Princes Risborough, Buckinghamshire HP27 9AA, UK.
Copyright © 1977 by the estate of Miles Hadfield. First published 1977, second edition 1988; reprinted 1997. Number 3 in the Shire Garden History series. ISBN 0 85263 919 8.

Printed in Great Britain by CIT Printing Services, Press Buildings, Merlins Bridge, Haverfordwest, Pembrokeshire SA61 1XF.

The cover photograph is of Vanbrugh's Temple of the Four Winds at Castle Howard, North Yorkshire. The photograph on the title page shows the monument to the first Duke of Marlborough in Capability Brown's landscape at Blenheim. Below, Stourhead Park, Wiltshire.

Contents

ACKNOWLEDGEMENTS

Illustrations are acknowledged as follows: John Anthony, page 15; Miles Hadfield, pages 8, 20, 26, 27, 28, 34, 35, 39, 41, 42, 45, 59, 64, 68; the Iris Hardwick Library, pages 2, 48, 67, 69; Cadbury Lamb, pages 1, 4, 7, 10, 19, 22, 31, 33, 46, 52-3, 54, 55, 56, 66 and cover; Department of the Environment, Crown Copyright, page 16; the National Gallery, page 36; the Stamford Mercury, page 61; Studio Aemaage, page 58; June J. Miller, page 62; British Tourist Authority, page 70.

The 'Praeneste' Arcade and the giant Apollo at Rousham.

Beginnings

Probably the first British garden constructed in what we should now call the grand manner was at Fishbourne near Chichester in West Sussex. It was not unearthed until the 1960s, when part of it was excavated. Created in about AD 75, it covered some 75,000 square feet and was in the style that was described in some detail by Roman writers such as Pliny the Younger, who lived at much the same time as the construction of the Sussex palace and had a famous garden in Tuscany with, it must be admitted, a view to the distant Appenines that was rather more exciting than the surrounds of Fishbourne.

But the fundamental principle of both gardens was the same. Their design was regular and balanced, the plan of each a piece of elaborate geometry designed with rulers, squares and compasses. There were evergreen trees and shrubs cut into the rigid shapes of topiary. Pergolas shaded paths from the sun — rather more necessary in Italy than Sussex. Ornate fountains played into rectangular sheets of water. Small buildings were carefully set so that one could rest in situations that commanded the view. Everything was firmly ordered and controlled. It was, indeed, regular and formal: the precursor of the present great and highly elaborate formal renaissance gardens still found in Italy from which later were developed the even more complex and lavish formal gardens of Le Notre in France.

So far, no other Roman gardens as large as Fishbourne have been found in Britain, but there are many traces of horticulture under the Romans.

Then, when the conquerors returned to the mainland of Europe, the inhabitants of Britain for centuries entirely neglected the creation of gardens as skilfully designed works of art.

Gardens became places for the cultivation of trees, shrubs and plants largely for utilitarian purposes. The introduction of plants from abroad for medicinal purposes developed the craft of horticulture, in which certain monastic orders — which were international — played an important part after the Norman conquest. But even so, if we accept the monastic gardens as being the largest and most consequential of their period, they must have been insignificant. At Evesham, out of a total of sixty servants, only three worked in the garden.

With the accession of Henry VII in 1485 ideas increasingly entered England from the Mediterranean regions. Perhaps the first great and grand garden created in England influenced by continental example that had descended from Rome was Cardinal Wolsey's at Hampton Court. Against the grandeur of this there was Sir Thomas More's Chelsea garden, with many choice and rare plants newly introduced from overseas. Gardening as a skilled craft and the careful design of gardens as something of an art had returned — inspired by the Mediterranean ideas of the Romans. To this day, the botanical names of garden plants are Latin.

English gardens, as they increased in numbers and often in size, were essentially formal in design — rigidly geometrical, tightly symmetrical (or skilfully balanced in their parts to appear so) and defying nature as the Romans had done. One authority, it is true, the great Francis Bacon, urged that a part of the thirty acres which he regarded as the correct size of a garden should be a heath, 'framed as much as may be to a natural wildness'. That was published in 1625, though written earlier. It is true that many formal gardens did include a so called 'wilderness', but they were fanciful designs studded with trees and far from Bacon's idea of being natural.

Gardens in the British Isles developed rapidly on these formal, artificial lines, with straight avenues. 'Planter John' Montagu had seventy miles of them at Boughton in Northamptonshire — as a principal feature, as were rectangular 'canals' of water, much topiary work and an abundance of small flower beds arranged in fanciful patterns (parterres), throughout the seventeenth and early eighteenth centuries. The firm of London and Wise, with large nurseries at Brompton supplying the necessary, usually clipped and trained trees and shrubs, dominated the scene. Vast gardens such as Chatsworth and Blenheim Palace were laid out in this manner: it was unthinkable that any garden, large or small, should be designed in other than this geometrical, formal manner. The inspiration latterly was the work of Andre Le Notre (1613—1700), working largely for his great patron, the 'Sun King', Louis XIV of France.

The style descended from the Roman originals, such as were once found on a small scale in England at Fishbourne. Le Notre's examples, and those in his style, still remain on the European continent and elsewhere.

But where are they now to be found in the British Isles, where they once abounded? They were destroyed from the early eighteenth century onward by the creation of the English landscape garden (which even went to France as *le jardin anglais!*). It is the only great aesthetic contribution made by the English — not even the Scots were involved — to the arts.

Robert Bakewell's wrought iron summerhouse at Melbourne Hall in Derbyshire.

That the destruction of the great, particularly eighteenth-century, formal gardens was vandalism equal to anything that happens today, and all in the name of art, cannot, alas, be denied. Two examples of the old style can still be seen and are open to the public. They are at Melbourne Hall in Derbyshire, designed by Henry Wise 'to suit with Versailles' (on a

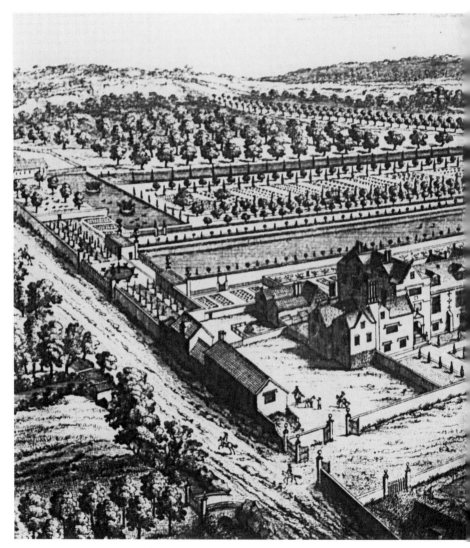

vastly smaller scale) and begun in 1696, and the National Trust's Westbury Court in Gloucestershire of the same date.

Westbury Court, Gloucestershire, in 1712.

A knot garden at Hampton Court, reconstructed on the site of an earlier garden.

Art and nature

As the English landscape garden is, unlike the formal garden, so closely connected with and inspired by Nature, it is interesting to comment on how the Englishman's views on the natural scene changed during the period we are discussing.

The cultured Englishman had from early times an undoubted fear of wild scenery, totally different from the feeling he developed in the eighteenth century and unbelievably different from that which most people hold today. That early view is justified by the surprisingly primitive nature and isolation of many parts of the countryside until the eighteenth century, and by the singular difficulties of communication with them. Our authors and poets particularly disliked the mountainous districts of the Continent, of which Marvell wrote in 1651:

> Here learn ye mountains more injust
> Which to abrupter greatness thrust,
> That do with your hook-shoulder'd height
> The Earth deform and Heaven fright.
> For whose excrescence ill design'd,
> Nature must a new centre find.

Dryden wrote: 'High objects, it is true, attract the sight, but it looks with pain upon craggy rocks and barren mountains'.

The Lake District was described as 'nothing but hideous hanging pooles and great pooles . . . . a man would think he were in another world', while as late as 1681 Charles Cotton described the Peak district as:

> Environ'd round with nature's shames and ills,
> Black heath, wild rock, bleak crags and naked hills.

In 1685 Sir William Temple advised gardeners on no account to follow the irregular, informal style of gardening practised by the Chinese for they would be sure to fail whereas it was twenty to one that they would succeed with the conventional formal manner.

While Le Notre and his followers were still the masters of the formal school in France, London (who died in 1713) and Wise (who was appointed gardener to Queen Anne in 1702) dominated garden design in the British Isles.

No murmur appears to have been raised, or at least published, against this state of affairs, and the universal acceptance of the formal, often grandiose, style of gardening and the wide displeasure of such uncivilised objects as mountains continued until Joseph Addison (1672—1719) published his *Remarks on Several Parts of Italy in the Years 1701, 1702, 1703.* He had been given a grant enabling him to travel on the Continent as training for the diplomatic service. Of the gardens he visited, he wrote:

> I have not seen any garden in Italy worth taking notice of. The Italians fall as short of the French in this particular, as they excel them in their palaces. It must, however, be said to the honour of the Italians, that the French took from them the first plans of the gardens, as well as of their waterworks; so that the surpassing of them is to be attributed to their riches rather than the excellence of their taste.

The term 'waterworks' was used to cover fountains, canals, formal pools, waterfalls and other such man-made ingenuities.

This attack on the very source of the design followed in the great English gardens of the day, though perhaps overlooked as the work of a precocious young Whig — the party which was later to support the new landscape movement — was shattering. Even more unfashionable was Addison's enjoyment of mountains and mountaineering. He gave a detailed and excited account of his ascent of Vesuvius.

There must have been a group of thinkers and philosophers working against the conception of the formal garden in the seventeenth century before the movement became well known by their writings that were put into practice in the first decades of the eighteenth century. Curiously, politics was concerned, for most belonged to the Whig party, which disliked the great power of the French monarchy.

Addison and Pope

The first of the best-known early attacks in widely read periodicals on the conventional Frenchified formal style of English gardens was made by Joseph Addison, urging a comparatively irregular confusion, in a letter addressed to the editor of *The Spectator* in its issue of 6th September 1712:

Having lately read your essay on The Pleasures of the Imagination, I was so taken with your thoughts upon some of our English gardens, that I cannot forbear troubling you with a letter upon that subject. I am one, you must know, who am looked upon as a humourist in gardening. I have several acres about my house, which I call my garden, and which a skilful gardener would not know what to call. It is a confusion of kitchen and parterre, orchard and flower-garden, which lie so mixt and interwoven with one another, that if a foreigner, who had seen nothing of our country, should be conveyed into my garden at his first landing, he would look upon it as a natural wilderness, and one of the uncultivated parts of our country. My flowers grow up in several parts of the garden in the greatest luxuriancy and profusion. I am so far from being fond of any particular one, by reason of its rarity, that if I meet with any one in a field which pleases me, I give it a place in my garden. By this means, when a stranger walks with me, he is surprised to see several large spots of ground covered with ten thousand different colours, and has often singled out flowers he might have met with under a common hedge, in a field, or in a meadow, as some of the greatest beauties of the place. The only method I observe in this particular, is to range in the same quarter the products of the same season, that they may make their appearance together, and compose a picture of the greatest variety. There is the same irregularity in my plantations, which run into as great a wilderness as their natures will permit. I take in none that do not naturally rejoice in the soil; and am pleased, when I am walking in a labyrinth of my own raising, not to know whether the next tree I shall meet with is an apple or an oak; an elm or a pear tree. My kitchen has likewise its particular quarters assigned it; for besides the wholesome luxury which that place abounds with, I have always thought a kitchen garden a more pleasant sight than the finest orangery, or artificial greenhouse. I love to see everything in its perfection; and am more pleased to survey my rows of coleworts and cabbages, with a thousand nameless pot-herbs, springing up in their full fragrancy and verdure, than to see the tender plants of foreign countries kept alive by artificial heats, or withering in an air and soil that are not adapted to them. I must not omit, that there is a fountain rising in the upper part of my garden, which forms a little wandering rill, and administers to the pleasure as well as the plenty of the place. I have so conducted it that it visits most of my plantations; and have taken particular care to let it run in the same manner as it would do in an open field, so that it generally passes through banks of violets and primroses, plats of willow or other plants, that seem to be of its own producing. There is another circumstance in which I am very particular, or, as my neighbours call me, very whimsical; as my garden invites into it all the birds of the country, by offering them the conveniency of springs and shades, solitude and shelter, I do not suffer any one to destroy their nests in the Spring, or drive them from their usual haunts in fruit-time; I value my garden more for being full of blackbirds than cherries, and very frankly give them fruit for their songs. By this means I have always the music of the season in its perfection, and am highly delighted to see the jay or the thrush hopping about my walks, and shooting before my eye across the several little glades and alleys that I pass through. I think there are as many kinds of gardening as of poetry; your makers of parterres and flower-gardens are epigrammatists and sonneteers in this art; contrivers of bowers and grottos, treillages and cascades, are romance writers. Wise and London are our heroic poets; and if, as a critic, I may single out any passage of their works to commend, I shall take notice of that part in the upper garden at Kensington, which was at first nothing but a gravel pit. It must have been a fine genius for gardening, that could have thought of forming such an unsightly hollow into so beautiful an area, and to have hit the eye with so uncommon and agreeable a scene as that which it is now wrought into. To give this particular spot of ground the greater effect, they have made a very pleasing contrast; for as on one side of the walk you see this hollow basin, with its several little plantations, lying so conveniently under the eye of the beholder, on the other side of it there appears a seeming

The Privy Garden at Hampton Court has been reconstructed on the foundations of the original garden laid out for William III.

mount, made up of trees, rising one higher than another, in proportion as they approach the centre. A spectator, who has not heard this account of it, would think this circular mount was not only a real one, but that it actually had been scooped out of that hollow space which I have before mentioned. I never yet met anyone who has walked in this garden, who was not struck with that part of it which I have here mentioned. As for myself, you will find, by the account which I have already given you, that my compositions in gardening are altogether after the Pindaric manner, and run into the beautiful wildness of nature without affecting the nicer elegancies of art. What I am now going to mention, will, perhaps, deserve your attention more than anything I have yet said. I find, that in the discourse which I spoke of in the beginning of my letter, you are against filling an English garden with evergreens; and indeed I am so far of your opinion, that I can by no means think the verdure of an evergreen comparable to that which shoots out annually, and clothes our trees in the summer season. But I have often wondered that those who are like myself, and love to live in gardens, have never thought of contriving a winter garden, which

The Queen's Garden at Kew is laid out as a seventeenth-century garden.

should consist of such trees only as never cast their leaves. We have very often little snatches of sunshine and fair weather in the most uncomfortable parts of the year, and have frequently several days in November and January that are as agreeable as any in the finest months. At such times, therefore, I think there could not be a greater pleasure than to walk in such a winter garden as I have proposed. In the summer season, the whole country blooms, and is a kind of garden; for which reason we are not so sensible of those beauties that at this time may be everywhere met with; but when Nature is in her desolation, and presents us with nothing but bleak and barren prospects, there is something unspeakably cheerful in a spot of ground which is covered with trees that smile amidst all the rigours of winter, and give us a view of the most gay season, in the midst of that which is most dead and melancholy. I have so far indulged myself in this thought, that I have set apart a whole acre of ground for the executing of it. The walls are covered with ivy instead of vines. The laurel, the hornbeam, and the holly, with many other trees and plants of the same nature, grow so thick in it that you cannot imagine a more lively scene. The glowing redness of the berries with which they are hung at this time, vies with the verdure of their leaves, and is apt to inspire the heart of the beholder with the vernal delight which you have somewhere taken notice of in your former papers. It is very pleasant, at the same time to see the several kinds of birds retiring into this little green spot, and enjoying themselves amongst the branches and foliage, when my great garden, which I have before mentioned to you, does not afford a single leaf for their shelter.

You must know, Sir, that I look upon the pleasure which we take in a Garden, as one of the most innocent delights in human life. A Garden was the habitation of our first parents before the fall. It is naturally apt to fill the mind with calmness and tranquillity, and to lay all its turbulent passions at rest. It gives us a great insight into the contrivance and wisdom of providence, and suggests innumerable subjects for meditation. I cannot but think the very complacency and satisfaction which a man takes in these works of Nature to be a laudable if not a virtuous habit of mind. For all which reasons I hope you will pardon the length of my present letter.

Perhaps even more famous is Alexander Pope's comic satire published in *The Guardian* during 1713:

We seem to make it our study to recede from nature, not only in the various tonsure of greens into the most regular and formal shape, but even in monstrous attempts beyond the reach of the art itself: we run into sculpture, and are yet better pleased to have our trees in the most awkward figures of men and animals, than in the most regular of their own . . .

A citizen is no sooner proprietor of a couple of yews, but he entertains thoughts of erecting them into giants, like those of Guildhall. I know an eminent cook, who beautified his country-seat with a coronation-dinner in greens, where you see the champion flourishing on horseback at one end of the table, and the Queen in perpetual youth at the other.

For the benefit of all my loving countrymen of this curious taste, I shall here publish a catalogue of greens to be disposed of by an eminent town-gardener, who has lately applied to me upon this head. He represents that for the advancement of a politer sort of ornament in the villas and gardens adjacent to this great city, and in order to distinguish those places from the mere barbarous countries of gross nature, the world stands much in need of a virtuoso gardener, who has a turn to sculpture, and is thereby capable of

improving upon the ancients in the imagery of evergreens. I proceed
to this catalogue:

Adam and Eve in yew; Adam a little shattered by the fall of the
tree of Knowledge in the great storm; Eve and the serpent very
flourishing.

Noah's Ark in holly, the ribs a little damaged for want of water.

The tower of Babel not yet finished.

St George in Box; his arm scarce long enough, but will be in a
condition to stick the dragon by next April.

A green dragon of the same, with a tail of ground-ivy for the
present.

NB — Those two are not to be sold separately.

Edward the Black Prince in Cypress. . . .

A Queen Elizabeth in Phyllirea, a little inclining to the Green
sickness, but of full growth. . . .

An old Maid of honour in wormwood.

A toppling Ben Johnson in Laurel.

Divers eminent modern poets in bays, somewhat blighted, to be
disposed of a penny worth. . . .

Pope also, in Epistle IV of his *Moral Essays*, wrote the famous lines on
the place of the natural landscape in garden design, with a reference to
the planning of the garden being created for Viscount Cobham at Stowe
in Buckinghamshire (now the site of the school):

> To build, to plant, whatever you intend,
> To rear the column, or the arch to bend,
> To swell the terrace, or to sink the grot,
> In all, let Nature never be forgot,
> But treat the goddess like a modest fair,
> Nor over-dress, nor leave her wholly bare;
> Let not each beauty everywhere be spied,
> Where half the skill is decently to hide.
> He gains all points who pleasingly confounds,
> Surprises, varies and conceals the bounds.
>   Consult the genius of the place in all:
> That tells the waters or to rise or fall;
> Or helps the ambitious hill the heavens to scale,
> Or scoops in circling theatres the vale;
> Calls in the country, catches opening glades,
> Joins willing woods, and varies shades from shades;
> Now breaks, or now directs, the intending lines;
> Paints, as you plant, and as you work, designs.

Topiary at Levens Hall in Cumbria.

> Still follow sense, of every art the soul,
> Parts answering parts shall slide into a whole,
> Spontaneous beauties all around advance,
> Start even from difficulty, strike from chance;
> Nature shall join you; Time shall make it grow
> A work to wonder at — perhaps a Stowe.
> Without it, proud Versailles! thy glory falls;
> And Nero's terraces desert their walls:
> The vast parterres a thousand hands shall make,
> Lo! Cobham comes, and floats them with a lake
> Or cut wide views through mountains to the plain,
> You'll wish your hill or shelter'd seat again.

Pope continues to throw abuse on the formal gardens. The parterre, with its masses of stonework, he describes as:

> The whole, a labour'd quarry above ground,
> Two cupids squirt before: a lake behind
> Improves the keenness of the northern wind.
> His gardens next your admiration call,
> On every side you look, behold the wall!

No pleasing intricacies intervene,
No artful wildness to perplex the scene:
Grove nods at grove, each alley has a brother
And half the platform just reflects the other.

The creator of this brilliantly abused formal design so strongly contrasted with that of Cobham at Stowe is named as Timon: when challenged to identify him, Pope refused.

This poem was published in 1733 and contains, in addition to the few lines quoted, some of the most telling and brilliant phrases that have ever been bandied about in the battle between the formal and natural schools of garden and landscape designers. Pope himself was a knowledgeable and enthusiastic practical horticulturist. His own small garden, its design and plants were well known to his contemporaries. Addison, on the other hand, was not much of a gardener himself.

A free stone wall over a yard high and an adjacent dry ditch combine to form a ha-ha.

Addison and Pope ignored

The writings of Addison and Pope, being part of the famous corpus of English literature, have been so often quoted that it is quite widely believed that they abruptly ended the domination of French formal design in England. Nothing is further from the truth. Not until 1712 was the first and last authoritative work on the French principles of garden design published in England (Le Notre himself did not die until 1700). This was an English translation by John James, the distinguished architect of Saint George's, Hanover Square, of the standard *La Theorie et la Pratique du Jardinage*, written by the Frenchman, d'Argenville. The French original was published in 1709 and the translation in 1712, its third edition appearing as late as 1743. There were no fewer than 236 subscribers to the original English translation, including most of the owners and creators of the famous gardens of the time. Its contents were also copied in the most important English gardeners' dictionary of the period.

We need not go into the details of d'Argenville's instructions, for a single plate from the book will show how totally distinct conventional designs were at the time of Addison and Pope's fulminations, and for decades after their deaths.

It is, however, almost impossible to find an old garden of this type in Britain today. Almost every old house with a garden built up to about 1735 was designed for a formal setting of this French style. But now it has gone — the movement and ideals set in motion by Addison, Pope and their fellow revolutionaries resulted in such a change in fashion that by degrees almost every example was eliminated.

There is one amusing point to note. Most writers on garden history attribute the invention of a boundary consisting of a dry ditch — the ha-ha — to Bridgeman. In fact it is a very old device. We have d'Argenville's description of it as translated by James: 'we frequently make through-views, called *Ah. Ah*, which are openings in the walls without grills, to the very level of the walks, with a large and deep ditch at the foot of them, lined on both sides to sustain the earth, and prevent the getting over, which surprizes the eye upon coming near it, and making one cry *Ah! Ah!*

from which it takes its name'.

As I have said, these formal gardens have almost disappeared from Britain. One example, albeit a good deal simplified, is Melbourne in Derbyshire. Laid out for Thomas Coke by the professional designers George London and Henry Wise from 1696 onwards, it was avowedly in the manner of Le Notre. We can still, in spite of the later alterations, see the fundamental French principles. The house stands a little raised above the garden on a terrace. At right angles to it is the broad and perfectly straight main axis of the garden. At first it crosses a lawn, where once there would have been the elaborate pattern of small flower beds and trimmed box bushes known as a parterre.

Next, after a drop down some steps, the path divides to pass either side of a small, elaborate pond at the centre of which, still on the main axis, is a fountain. And then on again to a famous piece of ironwork constructed by the smith Bakewell — it is an elaborate skeleton of a building. This too stands on the same rigid central axis, which then extends beyond the confines of the garden as a broad clearing through a wood until it disappears into the sky.

This main axis is frequently crossed at right angles by minor paths which lead to a variety of alleys, furnished with magnificent statuary, an occasional fountain, and in one place a sombre yew tunnel even older than the rest of the garden.

Except for the rich elaborate ornaments skilfully placed at vantage points, the ruler and compasses dominate the whole design.

At Westbury Court beside the river Severn in Gloucestershire the National Trust has saved the considerable remains of another garden, just as it was falling into decay. The date of the beginnings of this was, curiously, much the same as that of Melbourne. But though the ruler dominates its design even more rigidly, other features govern its use. The garden was created alongside a very old house and its length, owing to the restricted extent of the site, was limited. And the vistas, owing to the level ground and abundance of water, took the form of canals — as was not unusual at the time. Also the apex from which the principal of these was aligned was an exquisite red-brick pavilion, raised on white columns mounting to a glazed cupola on its roof. From within this there is a wide view, both over the garden and beyond, stretching over the flat estuarial countryside and to the Forest of Dean. (The builder of the pavilion, Duncombe Colchester, was a Commissioner of this royal forest, and so there might be a practical reason for the erection of this gem-like building, thus entitling it to be called a gazebo.)

Westbury Court is now in the hands of the National Trust. Few gardens display more succinctly and delightfully the essence of a formal garden, with close-clipped hedges outlining the water which replaces the grass

Opposite: Westbury Court.

and gravel of paths.

But gardens such as Melbourne and Westbury (Bramham in West Yorkshire is another) are but fragments of the style of British garden design which was general until the theories of Addison, Pope and their friends caused its obliteration from the scene; also, these gardens are on a very modest scale compared to a place such as was Canons on a site near Edgware acquired by James Brydges, later Duke of Chandos, in 1713. Canons and its creator are the thinly disguised subject of one of Pope's nastiest attacks, although Pope rather weakly denied that this was so. We have an unprejudiced account written by the traveller (and incidentally spy) John MacKay in 1722:

> There is a large terrace walk from whence you descend to the parterre; this parterre has a row of gilded vases on pedestals on each side down to the great canal, and in the middle, fronting the canal, is a gladiator, gilded also, and through the whole parterre was an abundance of statues as big as the life, regularly disposed. The greatest pleasure of all is that the divisions of the whole are only made by balustrades of iron and not by walls; you see the whole at once, be you in what part of the garden or parterre you will.

From other sources we learn that the grass seed was imported from Aleppo; 150 evergreen oaks were planted espalier-wise; fruit trees came from Jamaica, tortoises from Majorca; barrow ducks, storks, wild geese and cherry trees were imported, along with whistling ducks and flamingoes, from Antigua; ostriches and blue macaws wandered around; and eagles drank out of special stone basins.

The parterre employed during May sixteen men and two women; the turf was mown twice or three times weekly and weeded daily. The three main and perfectly straight avenues were respectively 1303 yards, 1000 yards and 808 yards long. The water was brought from Stanmore in two miles of elm pipes.

This vastness, rigidity and unnatural extravagance stood for everything that Addison and Pope despised. Though formality continued, never, it seems, did it recur on such an extravagant scale.

Indeed, Pope's own prophecy soon came true:

Another age shall see the golden ear
Imbrown the slope, and nod on the parterre,
Deep harvest bury all his pride has plann'd.
And laughing Ceres reassume the land.

Yet we should not forget that Humphry Repton, who will be discussed later, was destroying and 'improving' the remnants of old formal gardens and designing them afresh in the landscaped style almost until his death in 1818.

The Earl of Carlisle improves his landscape

The first professional gardener to accept something of the teachings of Addison and Pope and to bring nature into garden design seems to have been Stephen Switzer (1682—1745). In spite of his name, he is said to have been English, and possibly of gentlemanly stock, through some misfortune having had to turn his hand to gardening and writing.

He worked as a foreman in the Brompton nursery of London and Wise. Later, he wrote a number of books and had a nursery garden at Millbank and a stand at the sign of the Flower Pot in Westminster Hall. Incidentally, he waged war on the Scots gardeners who were then coming south in large numbers. He also worked in the north as a designer, particularly in Yorkshire, though he had been employed by Wise at Blenheim.

In his *Ichnographia Rustica* (1718) he particularly wrote on garden design, urging paths 'with as many twinings and windings as the villa will allow, diversifying the views, always striving that they may be so intermixed, as not to be all discerned at once.' He also wrote of 'that inexpressible somewhat to be found in the Beauty of Nature'.

In the same book he described how, when George London was planning the grounds for the third Earl of Carlisle's magnificent new building at Castle Howard, he had 'prescribed within Wray Wood a star which would have spoil'd the wood but that his Lordship's superlative genius prevented it and to the great advancement of the design has given it that labyrinth diverting model we now see it; and it is at this time a proverb in that place, York against London, in allusion to the design of a Londoner and Mr London the designer'. It is possible to elaborate this. The new Castle Howard was to have been built by the architect Talman, for whom the formalist George London usually designed the garden. Talman, however, fell out with his patron (which was not unusual) and was replaced in 1699 by the great and imaginative Vanbrugh. Presumably London went at the same time. There still exist the records of planting by the third Earl between 1705 and 1711; this suggests that Switzer's comment was not servile flattery but a genuine. tribute.

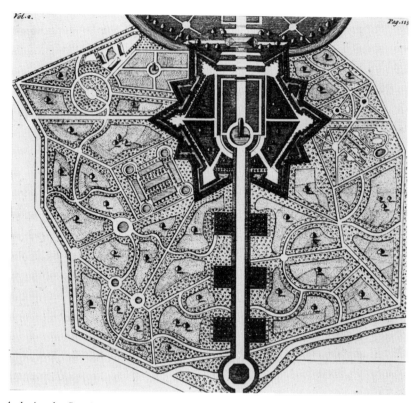

A design by Stephen Switzer for 'The manor of Paston divided and planted into Rural Gardens'.

But beyond this, a visit to the great park at Castle Howard introduces us to something new in our garden history — the design of a vast ornamental landscape, dominated by magnificent buildings set in grassy space sometimes planted with trees, a scene bearing no resemblance to the vast gardens such as Canons formerly made in the British Isles or elsewhere, and entirely different in conception from such gardens. (There have always been relatively small formal-style gardens by the house — but only as one incident in the overall scheme; those surrounding the fountain at present are by the nineteenth century designer Nesfield).

The setting of Castle Howard is an undulating, undramatic and immensely spacious scene, a pattern of fields and woods, giving a pleasant sensation that it is somewhat elevated above the rest of Yorkshire. The

Vanbrugh's Temple of the Four Winds at Castle Howard, North Yorkshire.

house, of great width and crowned with an ostentatious cupola, lies to one side of a very long avenue as straight and as formal as any avenue could be. The massive building is typical of the work of Vanbrugh in its weight and palace-like quality: it is quite devoid of any hint of English modesty. The long axis of the house remote from the avenue is continuous with a broad, slightly curving walk with Wray Wood a little above it on one side and overlooking the park on the other: because this pathway was originally a road it has an innate quality of inevitability and purpose. It leads to Vanbrugh's Temple of the Four Winds, which is a superb example of imaginative architecture, square, as befits its title, and architecturally related to the house.

The view seen from beside it is terminated by Hawksmoor's

The landscape at Castle Howard, with the bridge and Hawksmoor's Mausoleum.

mausoleum, a rotund, pillared, spikeless building of immense dignity and power, on high ground the other side of the shallow river valley. In front of it, the meandering stream is crossed by an arched 'Roman' bridge.

Elsewhere there are architectural features of merit but, though significant, they are of minor importance.

The whole, we may assume, was first adumbrated in 1699 when Vanbrugh took over. It took forty or so years to complete and was born in the imaginations of three men, Carlisle, Vanbrugh and Hawksmoor. It remains a conception purely of landscape: unlike most subsequent examples it is not overlain with legendary and historical allusions.

It is a singular and wholly original work, to which the word 'garden' can scarcely be applied. And we can see it today very much as it was at the time of its completion: an imagined landscape.

As a postscript to this account of Castle Howard, it is pleasant to emphasise the importance of native trees in the Earl's landscape, as suggested by his lines on a monument erected by him in 1731 to commemorate those he had planted between 1702 and that year:

> If to perfection these PLANTATIONS rise,
> If they agreeably my heirs surprise,
> This faithful pillar will their age declare
> As long as Time these Characters shall spare.
> Here then, with Kind Remembrance read his Name,
> Who for POSTERITY performed the same.

Stowe and Rousham

A very little later than Castle Howard the now famous landscape garden at Stowe was begun. It had similarities to Castle Howard, but its development was complex. Instead of just three men working on a simple theme, several people were concerned, two of them professional gardeners rather than architects or designers. Changes took place often, and what we see today is a mixture. But at the heart of it was Sir Richard Temple (1669—1749), created Viscount Cobham in 1718. He was a distinguished soldier under Marlborough and a politician, but much of his development of Stowe took place when he was politically out of favour.

The house never quite equalled Castle Howard in grandeur. Its landscape was not created in the same single-minded direction as was that at Castle Howard. Nor do we know to what extent Temple dominated those who worked for him — Bridgeman, Kent, Vanbrugh, Brown, Gibbs and others. The considerable studies that have lately been made of this remarkable place suggest that he was always very much the power behind the scenes.

Three of the men concerned were outstanding — Bridgeman, Kent and Brown. The first two did singular work at Stowe and their fame is bound up with the place, so they may well have their introduction here. 'Capability' Brown, as he became known, is about the only landscape gardener known to a wide public and will emerge in his solitary, if much imitated, glory and productivity later; there is now some doubt to what extent he was involved in the actual design — though he was certainly on the staff from 1740 (in the kitchen garden) until 1751.

Charles Bridgeman, who died in 1738—little is known about his birth and origins — was a key figure in the transition from the formal to the natural or landscape style of gardening. He was a brilliant surveyor and draughtsman, with a very considerable output of designs. He was a highly skilled practical gardener, at one time working for the firm of London and Wise; he eventually succeeded Henry Wise as gardener to Queen Anne, whose gardens were quite formal. He was a member of the St Luke's Club along with other outstanding artists and architects. For long he was best

known from Horace Walpole's reference to him in his observations on the
origins of landscape gardening:

> . . . the capital stroke, the leading step to all that has followed was
> (I believe the first thought was Bridgeman's) the destruction of walls
> for boundaries, and the invention of fosses — an attempt then
> deemed so astonishing that the common people called them Ha!
> Ha's! to express their surprise at finding a sudden and un-
> perceived check to their walk . . .
>
> I call a sunk fence the leading step for these reasons. No sooner
> was this simple enchantment made, than levelling, mowing and
> rolling followed. The contiguous ground of the park outside the
> sunk fence was to be harmonised with the lawn within; and the
> garden in its turn was to be set free from its prim regularity, that it
> might assort with the wilder country outside. The sunk fence
> ascertained the specific garden (i.e. immediately around the house),
> but that it might not draw too obvious a line of distinction between
> the neat and the rude, the contiguous out-lying parts came to be
> included in a kind of general design: and when nature was taken
> into the plan, under improvements, every step that was made,
> pointed out new beauties and inspired new ideas.

That is the type of layout that may still be seen round very many
country houses created from the mid eighteenth century onwards.

But Walpole's attribution to Bridgeman is only partly right. The ha-ha,
as we have seen, was in use much earlier in the old formal gardens,
deceiving the visitor into the belief that there was no rigid fence between
garden and landscape. It was, however, a device placed, according to
d'Argenville, at the end of a walk and performing its trick only across a
comparatively narrow gap in the high walls which surrounded the garden.
It thus, as it were, provided no more than a closely framed picture of a
carefully selected fragment of the surrounding countryside. Bridgeman's
ha-ha (perhaps Temple's military training in the use of entrenched sites
might also have been concerned) threw, or apparently threw, the whole of
the surrounding countryside — fields, woods, cattle, horses, sheep and all
— into the garden. This surrounding landscape could now be, or rather
was later to be, planted with trees and relieved with artificial sheets of
water to form a landscaped park, as distinct from the true park, an area
for hunting.

Bridgeman himself went only part way to reaching the logical
conclusion of the developments he initiated. He was brought up in the
tradition of our greatest formalists, George London and Henry Wise (and
it is now established that his work in this manner included gardens of
great importance) but his near contemporary Switzer, already mentioned,

Stowe, Buckinghamshire: the Palladian bridge at the end of what was originally the octagon lake.

the pioneer, if rather a tentative one, of the introduction of nature and the thoughts of philosophers and poets into garden design, said of him that his designs attempted an 'incomprehensible vastness' with a 'fancy that could not be bounded'.

Bridgeman (who like his friend Pope had never been to Italy) designed a remarkable new garden at Stowe, around a new house designed by Vanbrugh, to replace a very tight formal garden that had surrounded the old house. A feature was an octagonal lake. Vanbrugh and other architects scattered the scene with buildings, as the gardener would say, 'in variety', and many of these remain — an exquisite if amusing array of architect's specimens.

In 1733 Temple, now Lord Cobham, gave up his political activities and started a distinct new phase of Stowe's creation, which the late Christopher Hussey called pictorial.

It brings into the remarkable pageant of English garden artifice the final stage of its origins in the person of William Kent (1674—1748). At least, he was the practitioner of it. He was certainly under the influence of — possibly dominated by—the remarkable and immensely rich and powerful third Earl of Burlington (1694—1753), the great enthusiast for practising in England the architectural principles of the Italian Andrea Palladio (1518—80), who looked back even further to the great Roman architect and engineer, Vitruvius.

Burlington, like all his English contemporaries, made the Grand Tour down into Italy. There he studied architecture, the scenery and works of art, particularly the paintings of such artists as Poussin, Salvator Rosa, Albani and others. Their spacious landscapes of the Italian scene were scattered with the ruins of ancient buildings, to which were appended old allegories, the other properties often being wild rocks, and they were usually furnished with narrow cypress trees *(Cupressus sempervirens)* and the contrasting broad-headed stone-pines *(Pinus pinea)* — the closed and opened umbrellas of arboricultural writers. The light and the distances were superbly handled; the heat of the Mediterranean sun almost exuded from the canvasses; the vestibules within the porticoes of the ancient buildings displayed the only shade.

This dream-like world was saturating all men of wealth and taste, along with minor English artists on the look-out for commissions. Such was William Kent of Bridlington, then in Yorkshire (where Burlington was one of the wealthiest landowners), trained as a sign-painter but who had moved on from signs to pictures — not very good ones. In 1716 he met Burlington, who brought him back to London in 1719 and installed him in Burlington House. He designed objects from furniture to temples for Burlington and his friends; he knew all the right people, particularly Alexander Pope in the literary world. He was concerned with Burlington in the latter's Chiswick House of 1729 and its grounds.

But it is as a creator of the idea of the first true English landscape gardens, works of great art and singular originality, that Kent is famous.

All its origins are based precariously on the edge of the comic. Kent was no practical gardener (he suggested planting dead trees for effect). It was largely based on pictures — hence its 'picturesque' qualities. In these paintings of scenes furnished with buildings the hot Mediterranean sun with its bright light and clear-cut dark shadows — totally alien to England's moist skies — always shone. Classical legends and authors such as Virgil were ghosts haunting the scene and were essential to it — provided one was rich enough to have made the Grand Tour and learned something of them.

Lebanon cedars frame
Chiswick House, home of
the third Earl of Burlington,
who employed William
Kent to assist in designing
the house and grounds.

Right: The Temple of
Ancient Virtue which Kent
designed at Stowe.

Kent's Elysian Fields at Stowe, depicted in an eighteenth-century engraving.

The *deus ex machina*, Burlington, who made this possible, designed his Palladian-type villas to be set in this kind of natural landscape, not in the highly complex formal settings with which in ancient times they had been surrounded. In Britain we have not even the pines and cypresses essential to the Roman scene!

Only a highly skilled psychologist would be unwise enough to attempt an explanation of this world-famous phenomenon, known in French-speaking countries as *le jardin anglais*. But could he even begin to comprehend the working of the minds of Yorkshire's richest and most powerful aristocrat and, from the same county, a common sign-painter?

The conclusion of Bridgeman's tentative attempts at Stowe to allow the garden to become unconfined are plainly seen in Kent's alterations. He smoothed away many of Bridgeman's geometrical figures. He created the Elysian Fields, designing the famous Temple of Ancient Virtue on one side and the Shrine of British Worthies on the other.

But Kent's outstanding work at Stowe is confused by the presence of the creations of predecessors and successors; it can be seen more nearly in isolation at Rousham.

Before we discuss that gem, however, it is important to mention that

Lancelot ('Capability') Brown worked at Stowe from 1740 to 1751. He was for some years the practical gardener involved in all the developments. It has generally been assumed that latterly he was responsible for them, particularly when long sweeps of grass are concerned. But apparently this is now doubtful.

Kent never worked on a vast scale; apparently he never had the opportunity. And he might not have been successful. Rousham is, compared with Stowe, a very small garden.

Rousham House was at the time the home of the Dormers. The house stands on level ground above the river Cherwell near Steeple Aston in Oxfordshire. Bridgeman's plans for the garden around the house exist. Kent — who worked as architect and decorator on the house — extended and developed the garden, principally to the north-east of the house on a fairly steep and irregular bank whose base was the river. This did not form

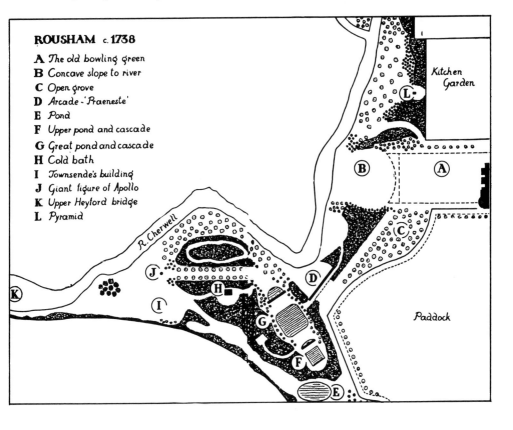

ROUSHAM c. 1738

A The old bowling green
B Concave slope to river
C Open grove
D Arcade - 'Praeneste'
E Pond
F Upper pond and cascade
G Great pond and cascade
H Cold bath
I Townsende's building
J Giant figure of Apollo
K Upper Heyford bridge
L Pyramid

Kitchen Garden

R. Cherwell

Paddock

anything like a straight boundary but had two right-angled bends, within the larger of which lay most of Kent's work, sloping in two directions, firstly in the broadest part down to the river and secondly lengthwise and narrowing down to Upper Heyford bridge, under which the river, in effect the theme of the garden, disappears. The house, above all this, does not overlook it but faces at right angles over to the far bank of the river where stands an 'eye catcher'.

Walking down the length of the garden, the building first encountered is an arcade, Praeneste. This stands at the base, as it were, of a broad avenue terminating at but not closed by a giant Apollo. On the left of this avenue is a demi-plantation of yew trees, enclosing a 'cold bath' and above that small ponds and cascades — a somewhat complex area heavily overhung with trees and branching into minor undulating vales. At its far end is a temple, named after its Oxford mason, Townende.

In the original planting conifers and flowering shrubs were frequently used, the former (as can often be seen in Kent's drawings) to replace the cypresses and pines of Rome, the latter to border the paths.

It remains one of the most individual and imaginative landscape garden designs in Britain.

'The Marriage of Isaac and Rebekah' by Claude is an example of the paintings that inspired the early landscape designers in England.

Woburn Farm, the Leasowes and a glimpse of Hagley

From patrician landscapes of the utmost grandeur we can turn to smaller places establishing a very much more widely based tradition in the English landscape manner.

Whereas we can visit Castle Howard and Stowe and are therefore able to grasp their significance, Woburn Farm and the Leasowes have, from our point of view, disappeared.

Philip Southcote (1699—1758) came of a Surrey Roman Catholic family. He was the nephew of Abbe Thomas Southcote, a friend of Pope. He was connected by marriage with Lord Petre (1713—43), a Catholic peer and close friend of the outstanding Quaker Peter Collinson, botanist, gardener and plant introducer who provided many new plants, trees and shrubs, for example to Hamilton at Painshill,. which is discussed later. Petre made one of the outstanding gardens of his day at Thorndon in Essex, planting on a vast scale. He was first and foremost a horticulturist and arboriculturist and was not, apparently, interested in the landscape movement.

Southcote called himself an *eleve* of Petre. In about 1735 he acquired Woburn (or Wooburn) Farm near Weybridge. He had the idea of combining the new style of gardening with farming. Shortly after Southcote died — the garden remaining in the hands of his widow — Whateley gave this description:

> A sense of the propriety of such improvements about a seat, (Whateley had discussed the natural beauties of a farm and its buildings), joined to the more simple delights of the country, probably suggested the idea of an *ornamented farm*, as the means of bringing every rural circumstance within the verge of a garden. . . The place contains a hundred and fifty acres, of which near five and thirty are adorned to the highest degree; of the rest, about two-thirds are in pasture, and the remainder is in tillage: the decorations are, however, communicated to every part; for they are disposed along the sides of a walk, which, with its appendages, forms a broad

belt around the grazing grounds; and is continued, though on a more contracted scale, through the arable. This walk is properly the garden; all within it is farm.

(The ornamented farm became known in genteel circles as the *Ferme Orne*. The Reverend W. Mason in *The English Garden* (1772) wrote: 'Mr Southcote was the introducer, or rather the inventor of the *Ferme orne* (sic), for it may be presumed that nothing more than the term is of French extraction.')

There were buildings on the walks which were of considerable attraction: an octagonal structure, the ruin of a chapel, a neat Gothic building by the house, and 'other objects of less consequence, little seats, alcoves, and bridges, continually occur' (William Kent was concerned with some of these).

> The lowings of the herds, the bleating of the sheep, and the tinkling of the bell-wether, resound thro' all the plantations; even the clucking of poultry is not omitted; for a menagerie of a very simple design is placed near the Gothic building; a small serpentine river is provided for the water-fowl; while the others stray among the flowering shrubs on the banks, or straggle about the neighbouring lawn: and the corn fields are the subjects of every rural employment, which arable land, from seed time to harvest, can furnish.

Here indeed was a mingling of nature, farming and artifice. Whateley did admit that the simplicity of a farm was wanting among such a profusion of ornament and that a rusticity of character could not be preserved amidst all the elegant decorations which may be lavished on a garden.

We do not hear much about the later history of this remarkable place, though J. C. Loudon reported that, about a century after it was begun, it contained one of the largest liquidambar trees in England, a remarkably fine hemlock spruce, very large tulip trees, acacias, hickories, pines, cedars, cypresses and a magnificent cut-leaved alder.

If Southcote's Woburn Farm is now forgotten, the Leasowes Farm, although it has disappeared, is still remembered. William Shenstone (1714—63) was a charming if minor poet and so subject, as a literary person, to not infrequent mention by the over-numerous students of English literature; his consequential essay *Unconnected Thoughts on Gardening* remains unread by modern landscapers who should be concerned with it. The Leasowes was not far from Birmingham and the Black Country, quite close to the famous park of George Lyttleton at Hagley. When it became well-known his farm became the objective of many 'Sunday starers' and was inevitably visited and commented upon by

Philip Southcote's 'ferme ornee' at Woburn near Weybridge.

Samuel Johnson with Mrs Thrale and others of that type.

The garden has disappeared but its broad setting, now covered by a golf course and sprayed over by suburbia, remains unchanged. It lies beneath the modest Clent Hills on the ground indicated markedly by the fall of the road down Mucklow's Hill, which shows the descent from the Birmingham plateau to the lower lands spreading to the borders of Wales.

Shenstone — who was a truly provincial Englishman, despising the Grand Tour as much as he admired the classics and their legends — made his garden in the form of a winding circuit in and around his property. Seats were placed at suitable stopping points, each with an appropriate motto. The path was scattered with urns, obelisks and trophies engraved with memorial verses to his friends; piping Pans and other suitable sculptures terminated the vistas down the glades. At the highest point in the grounds could be seen, at a 'prodigious distance', looking westward, the mountains of Wales, which finished the scene 'most agreeably'.

Richard Dodsley, Shenstone's publisher, in 1764 published a map of the grounds. It is a little optimistic, for he mentions that some of the 'waterworks' remained uncompleted and admits that the so-called cascades were not Niagaras.

The principal features of this plan are shown in the simplified reproduction (page 41), which indicates the very irregular nature of the paths and suggests the extremely undulating ground.

The winding lane (1) leads to the estate, on which there was no walk. One can go down to a small pool (2) which is linked to five other smaller pools. Beyond them is a curious little building (3) made from the roots of old trees; within it was a tablet bearing several verses hinting at the fairy-like nature of the scene, with the final one rather more astringent:

> And tread with awe these favour'd bowers,
> Nor wound the shrubs, nor bruise the flowers;
> So may your path with sweets abound
> So may your couch with rest be crown'd!
> But harm betide the wayward swain,
> Who dares our hallow'd haunts profane!

From here the house (4) is seen, divided from the fields by a ha-ha. Near a wood are the ruins of a medieval priory (5) and a large sheet of water (6) 'almost a lake'. Next, the path crosses a stream below 'the fairy vision' of a cascade (7), with the steeple of Halesowen church seen as a feature through the trees. A seat (8) is placed to give a view of the ruined priory, while another seat (9) is set to look upon a distant object like an Egyptian pyramid, which is, however, the smelting house of a glassworks. At (10) is a giant goblet inscribed with this old Shropshire toast: *To all friends around the Wrekin* — the singularly shaped hill visible in the distance on a clear day. A wicket gate (11) opens into a path through wilder ground and branching from it is a lovers' walk (12) reaching another pool. Another seat is at (13). Coming back down the valley, a wood of deep gloom and quiet, Virgil's Grove, is at (14). Behind the house is a shrubbery (15).

Shenstone's own views on his gardening at the Leasowes may be epitomised in the opening words of his *Unconnected Thoughts on Gardening*:

> Gardening may be divided into three species — kitchen gardening — parterre gardening — and landskip, or picturesque gardening: which latter is the subject intended in the following pages — It consists in pleasing the imagination by scenes of grandeur, beauty or variety. Convenience has no share here; any further than it pleases the imagination.

Though not strictly a *ferme ornée*, it is not inappropriate to include here the park at Hagley, lying on somewhat steeply undulating land a few miles to the south-west of the Leasowes, and the home of George (later Baron) Lyttleton (1709—73). He was a politician, writer and friend of Pope,

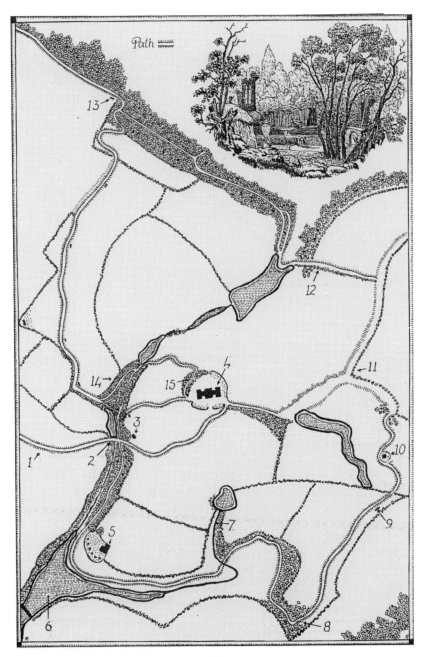

Path ░░░░

13

12

11

14

15

3

2

1

10

5

7

9

6

8

The Leasowes (see text opposite for key).

Hagley: the ruined castle and a Lebanon cedar planted in 1751.

Addison and James Thomson, author of *The Seasons.* As a poet he is perhaps remembered for the *Monody on the Death of His Wife,* which event seems to have turned him to landscaping his park as a distraction. This began with the building on a high point of a ruined castle designed by the squire-architect from the Cotswolds, not far away, Sanderson Miller. This was in 1747. Today it still stands dramatically, cattle grazing around it, not far from a Lebanon cedar planted in 1751 in a spot most effectively chosen by Lyttleton. (He was a keen planter of ornamental trees as part of his landscape, going to some trouble to ensure that they were rightly placed.)

Another delightful and remarkable building is the copy of the temple of Theseus in the Doric manner by James Stuart. Built in 1751 it is one of the earliest examples of this style in England.

Another feature of some consequence is the slim column honouring Frederick, Prince of Wales — a most unpopular figure in history books but of consequence in the history of landscape. Lyttleton was his secretary, while others who were associated with him were Hamilton of Painshill and William Kent, who altered his garden which later became part of the botanic gardens at Kew.

Not the least significant feature today of Hagley is the view from its idyllic acres of the still pregnant but changing Black Country lying not far away; yet, with a turn of the head, the richly fertile west Midlands can be seen disappearing into the Welsh borders.

Painshill

In 1738 the Hon. Charles Hamilton (1704-86), fourteenth child and the ninth and youngest son of James, sixth Earl of Abercorn, acquired the lease of land at Painshill in Surrey.

First, we shall try and give some account of Hamilton, who was to convert this land into one of the most remarkable landscape gardens, planted in an original manner, in England. This is almost impossible, for his books, papers and correspondence, which should have descended in the family along with documents of his heir — which are duly in place — are not now present. Unlike the creation of many other gardens, we have no first-hand account of the origins of Painshill, nor Hamilton's views on his objectives. Fortunately, these stand out from the numerous, if occasionally puzzling, descriptions recorded by visitors.

Hamilton was at Christ Church, Oxford, graduating in 1723. Among his contemporaries and friends were Stephen Fox, later Lord Ilchester, and his brother Henry, later Lord Holland. He was in Rome, where his portrait was painted, as a young man, and then held a post under Frederick, Prince of Wales, and so was closely in touch with another 'landscaper', Lord Lyttleton, who was the Prince's secretary. He banked with Hoare's bank (from which he borrowed heavily) and so was well acquainted with Henry Hoare, a year older, whose type of garden buildings he also raised, with the important difference that, while the distinguished architect Flitcroft worked with Hoare, a very minor architect — and possibly Hamilton himself — seems to have designed the Painshill structures.

Frederick, Prince of Wales, was closely connected with the intellectuals of the gardening world of his day, and his widow, the Princess Augusta, was virtually the creator of what eventually became the present Kew gardens. The influences on design, as we have seen, were Claude, Gaspar Poussin and Salvator Rosa.

Hamilton had, therefore, all the background of antiquarian aesthetics, taste and style of the pioneer landscapers, but he possessed qualities they did not have. He was a practical gardener and farmer — his experiments with his vineyard and winemaking are known. He took steps to improve the fertility of his barren gravel soil. And not only did he form a lake which was a principal feature of his landscape, but he himself (so it is said) invented the pump that filled it from the neighbouring river.

An early description of the place described it as being 'situated on the utmost verge of a moor, which rises above a fertile plain, watered by the river Mole. Large valleys descending in different directions towards the river break the brow into separate eminences; and the gardens are extended along the edge, in a semicircular form, between the winding river which describes their outward boundary, and the park which fills up the cavity of the crescent; the moor lies behind the place, and sometimes appears too conspicuously: but the views on the other side into the cultivated country are agreeable; they are terminated by hills at a competent distance'.

Whereas Southcote created an 'ornamental farm', Hamilton produced an ornamental park — including a lake of no less than thirty acres whose water was pumped up from the river. It was a great undertaking.

The buildings he erected included a Gothic tent, which 'in point of lightness few buildings could exceed'. The bridge 'turns out to be the covering of a most beautiful grotto . . . under it is a large encrustation of fossils, and spar everywhere hanging like icicles has a most pleasing effect. On each side of the water is a small path, parted from the stream by marine fossils. Nothing can have a more elegant effect than the ceiling of this grotto (in which is stuck, with great taste, a profusion of spar) hanging over the water, as if a kindred, but congealed nature'.

A most interesting thing was that Hamilton had set, within a secreted space, an old-fashioned parterre and orangery, where during summer exotic plants were bedded out intermixed with common shrubs to provide a constant succession of flowers.

Hamilton delighted in visitors, for low chairs drawn by small horses could be hired by them from inns at Cobham to go over his grounds.

It is pleasing to recall what Uvedale Price, that keen and rather severe critic of his contemporaries and predecessors, wrote of Painshill in 1796:

> I have always understood that Mr Hamilton, who created Painshill, not only had studied pictures, but had studied them for the express purpose of improving real landscape. The place he created (a task of quite another difficulty from correcting or from adding to natural scenery) fully proves the use of such a study. Among many circumstances of more striking effect I was highly pleased with a walk which leads through a bottom skirted with wood; and I was pleased with it, not from what *had*, but from what had *not* been done; it had no edges, no borders, no distinct lines of separation; nothing was done, except keeping the ground properly

The lake created by Charles Hamilton at Painshill in Surrey.

neat, and the communications free from any obstruction. The eye and the footsteps were equally unconfined; and if it is a high commendation to a writer or a painter that he knows when to leave off, it is not less to an improver (landscaper).

It is significant that Price was, as we shall see, one of the first important writers to suggest the planting of rhododendrons and similar gay shrubs and trees in woodlands. Perhaps he gained the idea from what he saw at Painshill.

Finally, it is pleasant to quote that experienced connoisseur of gardens, Mrs Montagu, who wrote in 1755:

I think it is a most agreeable place to live in; there may be others who have in a higher degree any one of the perfections there, but surely there is not any, where so many meet; like a well accomplished companion, it has something to please one in every disposition, and from variety of talents never wearies . . . nothing is forced, nothing seems artificial, but art has been only to the place . .

It is generally assumed that Charles Hamilton had to abandon Painshill because he had spent so much on it. He remarked, too, on the strain of planning and running the estate, to which it is clear he devoted great energy. In 1773 it was taken over by a new owner, who began the series of alterations that have since taken place. Hamilton moved to Bath, where he died in September 1786.

A number of more or less contemporary general descriptions of Painshill were published. But of particular interest are the detailed references to many of the rare and new conifers grown there in A. B. Lambert's *A Description of the Genus Pinus* (1803 on) and to other trees and shrubs in J. C. Loudon's *Arboretum et Fruticetum Britannicum* (1838).

Hamilton was the true venturous pioneer of the modern landscape garden, adorning the poetically and aesthetically inspired landscape not with the usual conventional trees but with those exotics coming in steadily increasing numbers from overseas, particularly the American continent, which have subsequently modified not only our gardens but our landscape.

The ruined abbey at Painshill.

Stourhead

It is not possible to place this wonderful garden in a neat position historically. Briefly, it was first created as a landscape around a man-made lake furnished with representations of historic buildings set among mostly native woodland trees. Then, some sixty years later, a transformation was begun by decorating — indeed, rather more than decorating — the whole area by planting exotic trees, a process that has continued to this day and has entirely altered, so far as we know, the original conception of the place.

The Hoare family had built up a successful banking business: In 1717 the estate around Stourton in Wiltshire was acquired by a Henry Hoare (1677-1725). Soon the old house was pulled down and a new one built, designed by Colen Campbell, a pioneer of the Palladian style. It is the same house that now stands there, somewhat altered, and was named Stourhead, for the simple reason that it overlooked the valley at whose head were the springs which were the source of the stream that became the river Stour. Like much of the country around, the valley must then have been rather bare.

This Henry Hoare had a son, another Henry (1705-85), who, to distinguish him from his father, was called 'the magnificent'. He was, indeed, distinguished in every way and a student of literature, particularly of contemporary authors. He travelled in Italy and saw the scenery of the Romans and the pictures of Claude and his period (he could, however, only buy copies of the paintings). Moreover, he knew the Duchess of Queensbury's gardens at Amesbury, where Bridgeman worked from 1738. He moved into the new house at Stourhead, and his work on turning the valley into a famous work of pure landscape art was soon begun. It was, perhaps, partly inspired as a distraction (comparable with Lyttleton's Hagley) from the melancholy caused by the death of Henry's second wife in 1743.

In about 1741 the youthful streams of the Stour were merged to form the lake, a complete transformation of the valley. Trees were planted on

Stourhead: the Pantheon (above) and the Bristol High Cross (opposite).

the hillsides, not as specimens but as contrived masses of contrasting
greens and textures; the trees predominantly used were the beech and the
common silver fir (an odd, unnatural mixture). But more important was
the engagement as architect of Henry Flitcroft (1697-1769), a protege of
Lord Burlington and also an architectural historian. In the years that
followed, a series of buildings, mostly with allusions to classical

architecture, arose around the lake, disclosed one after another as one proceeds. Many look on beautifully disposed views, such as that over the lake from the Pantheon. There are other buildings rather remote from classical allusions, such as Alfred's Tower, for historical reasons recalling Alfred the Great, a British hero fighting for freedom. Another monument unconnected with Virgilian legend was the Bristol High Cross, reconstructed from its fragments which had lain in the crypt of Bristol cathedral and were presented to Stourhead by the Dean. This was among the early symptoms of a change in taste towards the 'Gothick'.

It is pleasant today on a sunny spring noon to sit on the steps of the Pantheon, feeling a little irreverent that the effusive classicism of so honoured an exquisite replica of antiquity should be so treated, and watch a silver swan on the lake and the first swallow clipping the water with its wings. But it is also a little odd, for a few yards away is the Gothic cottage! Disregarding the leafless trees, we see the lake and its banks as a superbly formed landscape, but Henry Hoare's incongruously mixed buildings (particularly as few of us now know the significance of their originals), delightful if absurd, seem perhaps to be a pioneering surrealist landscape. It was certainly not a garden as we understand it, planted with ornamental trees, shrubs and flowers. It was bare of these furnishings at the time of Henry the Magnificent's death. He had retired to a villa at Clapham designed by Flitcroft, and there he died in 1785.

The property was left to his grandson, Richard Colt Hoare (1758-1838). Upset by the death of his wife, a Lyttleton, in 1785, he did not live at Stourhead but spent much of his time abroad. He was a celebrated antiquarian, his studies centred in Italy, North Wales and Wiltshire. Ultimately he returned to Stourhead in 1791 and made certain alterations to the house and the plan of the garden which largely gave them their present form. Above all, he was an ardent botanist and gardener, and in 1791 and 1792 he made considerable arboricultural plantings around the lake, thus initiating the second phase of Stourhead and entirely altering the setting of the lake and buildings. The planting that he began was continued by his successors, covering the important periods of introductions from abroad — from western North America, from Japan and from north-west China.

Many of the trees now growing are among the finest in Britain. Their variation in form and foliage is prodigious, their placing done with great thought and imagination. To visit Stourhead on a sunny day in autumn when the exotic deciduous trees are blazing, the conifers rigid and in every shade of green, all arising from Henry Hoare's great and very English landscape scattered with his — or perhaps we should say predominantly Flitcroft's — architectural fantasies, provides an emotional experience that cannot be found elsewhere in the world.

'Capability' Brown and Mr Repton

Lancelot Brown (1715—83) has already been mentioned as gardener — perhaps more — at Stowe. He was born at Kirkharle in Northumberland. The local school was good and he took full advantage of it. At sixteen he entered the garden of Sir William Loraine nearby and learned to be a practical, professional gardener — a skill usually unknown to the arbiters of garden aesthetics. In 1739 he moved to Wotton, the estate owned by Sir Richard Grenville, brother-in-law to Lord Cobham of Stowe, which was only fourteen miles away. Brown moved to Stowe in 1740, working in the kitchen garden at first and eventually becoming head gardener at a time still pregnant with the new ideas of landscaping: perhaps he actually was responsible for design there in the last years of Cobham, who died in 1749. Certain it is that his employer allowed him to design landscapes for other owners, and, for example, he submitted plans for Packwood in Warwickshire in 1751, the year he left Stowe and set up in London as the immensely successful 'Capability' Brown. He travelled on horseback from one usually aristocratic and always wealthy client to another. After a mounted reconnaissance, it is said, he would report to his client that the estate had 'capabilities of improvement' — hence his name. He became very friendly with the Holland family, famous builders, a mutually useful friendship, particularly when Miss Brown married young Henry Holland, the up and coming architect.

Brown as a consultant was an obliging one. He was immensely ingenious, particularly in planning his usually glorious lakes: the famous lake at Blenheim he conjured out of an insignificant stream, the Glyme. It was over this puny trickle that Vanbrugh threw his great triumphal bridge, designed to be on a scale commensurate with the Duke of Marlborough's victories. Brown's genius later raised the water to a level that justified the massiveness of the structure crossing it.

For the Earl of Coventry his skill with water took on another aspect. He turned the marshy, worthless land where the Avon joins the Severn at Croome into an undulating landscape of great beauty, confining the uncontrolled waters of the swamp within a lake.

Blenheim: Vanbrugh's bridge, flooded by Capability Brown's artificial lake. Previous pages: The view from the south front at Stowe.

His planting, however, was stereotyped and lacked genius; as Horace Walpole said, men would take it for the work of nature. His parks were bounded by a sinuous band of trees to screen them. The paths and drives were equally sinuous; they never approached their objective directly. Trees were arranged carefully in clumps. The mansion was closely confined within a ha-ha; the garden proper (and it was a period of greatly increasing skill in horticulture) was confined within high walls and discreetly concealed from the windows of the house. The trees used were the British natives — oak, ash, beech, sometimes Scots pine. It seems the only exotic that Brown liked was the Lebanon cedar.

Today, the destruction of timber in two world wars, by reckless road making and ill-considered housing estates has made the preservation of every Brown landscape a matter of importance. (By replacing worn-out trees as necessary, which is not difficult, they can be maintained for the future.)

But Brown and his assistants and imitators have a black mark against them. The great formal gardens of the age of London and Wise were, with

The view of the Thames from the terrace of Nuneham Courtenay in Oxfordshire.

few exceptions, obliterated under their commands. London's famous gardens around the palace at Blenheim were destroyed in the making of Brown's park. (But a replacement by a French architect was made much later.) How many avenues were cut down is not recorded: one of the very few in a Brown landscape that survives is at Charlecote in Warwickshire, where the Lucy of the time refused to let Brown have his way.

In February 1783 Brown went to call on his close friend and patron Lord Coventry at his London house. On returning to his house at Hampton Court which he now held as Royal Gardener, he collapsed and died.

It has been estimated that Brown was responsible for the design of 170 gardens, nearly all in his stereotyped style. His former assistants and imitators — the names of Haverfield, Spyers, Woods, Webb and Emes are known in this connection — were also very Brown-like in their achievements.

Brown at his most imaginative and very best can be seen at Blenheim. The National Trust has Berrington in Herefordshire and Charlecote in

Attingham Park in Shropshire.

Warwickshire. Nuneham Courtenay in Oxfordshire can be seen from the Thames; it includes a flower garden designed by the Reverend William Mason, a protagonist of Brown in his quarrel with Sir William Chambers, the architect.

His landscapes were predominantly in the Home Counties and the Midlands. Not infrequently, they spread over land not well suited to agriculture. The production of timber was often a consideration — which benefited the owners financially if not aesthetically in two world wars.

But today we must hold Brown and his fashion to blame for the destruction of very many of the formal gardens designed particularly to suit our finest surviving houses built before about 1700.

When 'Capability' died, the several landscapers working in the manner that he had popularised and in which he had become dominant must (we can surely assume) have been expecting that his practice and the wide fashion that it had set would fall into their hands.

But they were quite wrong. Humphry Repton (1752—1818) — a name almost as well-known today as that of Brown — appeared from nowhere.

At the time of his death he had probably landscaped more parks than Brown himself.

His father, John, was a prosperous collector of taxes; his mother came from a respected Suffolk family. He was born at Bury St Edmunds and went to the local grammar school, which he disliked. His parents moved to Norwich and he went to school there. His father had inside knowledge about the relative prosperity of the trades and professions, and it was decided that Humphry would do well as a merchant dealing with Holland. So off he went to that country to finish his education, living in the home of Zachary Hope, a wealthy and cultivated man. The consequence was that Humphry, by nature accomplished, became versed in the continental graces. His letters show him to have been interested in the arts and also Dutch gardening. This surprised him, as it consisted of parterres with dwarf hedges filled not with plants but with glittering minerals such as brick dust, coal, broken glass and so on to make a gay, sparkling pattern. He was a skilful flautist, had a talent for sketching and, indeed, was adept at all the genteel arts.

On his return he married and set up as a merchant. However, he did not succeed as his father had prophesied. So he next set up as a country gentleman, living at Sustead near Aylsham in Norfolk. A schoolfellow, James Edward Smith (1759—1828), later founder of the Linnean Society (he was knighted in 1814) encouraged his interest in botany. His neighbour, William Windham of Felbrigg, with a famous library, encouraged his interests in the arts and sciences. He became interested in history and architecture, making drawings of the seats of the local gentry.

In 1783 Windham, appointed to a government position in Dublin, took Repton with him as confidential secretary. Windham, however, resigned and came home, leaving Humphry in charge. Thus he came to know well numerous persons of high social and political standing; in turn, he became known as a man of great charm and capability.

He returned home and settled down at Hare Street near Romford. He developed his garden.

But more consequential, he financed a business venture which failed; no longer was he a gentleman of independent means. Further, he was middle-aged.

It is said that his anxieties ended in the middle of one sleepless night. 'Capability' Brown had just died; there was no one upon whom the mantle of successor would automatically descend. His interests had given him a considerable knowledge of historical architecture; through his friend J. E. Smith and his own practical interest in making his own garden he had an unusually expert knowledge of horticulture, while his talent as an amateur artist was considerable. But even more important, he had accumulated a considerable number of friends within the social category that would have

W. Holl fe

engaged Brown to improve their gardens had he not died.

So he wrote to many of these friends offering his services as an improver of the landscapes around their houses. He was soon successful. Great landowners such as the Duke of Portland at Welbeck engaged his services. He worked at Cobham in Kent and Ashridge in Hertfordshire. He was a great success, at first producing landscapes whose principles of design were much the same as those followed by Brown at the time of his death. (Indeed, Brown's son Lancelot — by now a member of Parliament — lent him his father's papers.)

There were, however, considerable differences. Brown, perhaps, became sophisticated through experience. Repton was sophisticated from the start. He was highly educated, a talented draughtsman, and had been abroad. He had acquired a considerable knowledge of historical architecture.

We know Brown only by his works, the many plans he produced for his clients and correspondence concerning them (he was quite willing to alter his ideas to suit their own whims). We have anecdotes, for example, of his political intermediacy between clients of different political views. And we have his surviving landscapes. But they show little evidence of having descended from Burlington, Kent and the Italian campagna as seen in the Italian painters.

We know a great deal about Repton as a landscape designer. It is no

Opposite:
Humphry Repton
was a worthy
successor to
Capability Brown.

Right: Repton's
original planting
at Garnons in
Herefordshire.

exaggeration to say that Brown was primarily concerned with the landscape outside the environs of the house, while Repton (as a man highly sensitive to social ranks and proprieties) considered the setting of the mansion within the landscapes to be of great consequence. On visiting a client, he made a very thorough study of the scene, with careful sketches. From these, he produced a picture of the scene as it was. Then he made a second drawing of the scene as it would be if he were honoured with the commission to 'improve' it, including architectural alterations to the mansion if necessary. (He was for a time in partnership with John Nash, the architect. A good early example of Repton's work is the park at Attingham in Shropshire, a National Trust property he designed in 1797, the earlier George Steuart house having a picture gallery designed by Nash.) By 1806 he had produced three thousand sketches in the course of his work.

Repton also wrote freely on his theories; his *Observations on the Theories and Practice of Landscape Gardening,* published 1803 with coloured aquatints, is a magnificent work. Of great interest is the small *An Enquiry into Changes in Landscape Gardening* published in 1806 as an answer to an attack on his and in particular Brown's work by 'Mr Knight's' and 'Mr Price's' publications.

From it, we learn that:

> . . . the English garden became the universal fashion. Under the great leader, Brown, or rather those who patronised his discovery, were we taught that nature was to be our only model. He lived to establish a fashion in gardening, which might have been expected to endure as long as nature should exist . . . Brown *copied nature,* his illiterate followers *copied him.*

So much for the place of Burlington and Kent, under whose aegis Brown worked for so long!

Likewise, Repton is very insistent that the picturesque has no place in garden landscapes. That word he uses in its once correct English meaning — resembling a picture. In other words, the inspiration of the painters who inspired Burlington, Kent, Temple, Hoare and others who brought back their ideas, and where possible their pictures, from the Grand Tour to develop the English landscape was to be ignored.

Fortunately, however, in spite of all his theorising he produced a great many calm and desirable English park landscapes — and his imitators many more — which are maintained to this day.

Burghley House, near Stamford, stands in another of Brown's landscapes.

But the brilliant landscape tradition which still flourishes and was created by men such as Hamilton at Painshill and revived by Mr Knight and Mr Price, against whom Repton inveighed, is of more consequence today.

Mr Knight, Mr Price and after

These two Herefordshire squires attacked by Repton in so gentle and genteel a manner (which they scarcely deserved) brought the landscape garden back on to the lines first put into practice by Hamilton at Painshill: a rich variety of planting was employed and much was drawn from the pictures of great artists — that is, the designs were picturesque within the true meaning of the word. Neither, however, had any enthusiasm for imitative ornamental buildings in their designs, other than in the great variety of styles followed both inside and out of their mansions.

Both lived in the hilly and, in modern terms, picturesque parts of Herefordshire. It was not the sort of terrain in which Brown's and Repton's landscapes were typically set. But Brown's Moccas, beside the Wye, Berrington and Oakley Park were not far away, while Repton's Garnons was virtually beside Price's Foxley.

Repton's Mr Knight was Richard Payne Knight (1750-1824), a member of a very prosperous family of ironmasters which, having denuded England's first Black Country — in the district where Telford New Town now stands — of timber, moved south to pillage the forests of north Herefordshire. He was widely travelled, deeply cultured and best known internationally as an authority on and collector of classical antiquities — his famous collection was bequeathed to the British Museum.

In about 1772 he began building Downton Castle, a mock medieval building with an interior in the ancient Greek manner. It can be seen today — though now rather larger and with an extra tower added — from the rough road that winds along below, beside the river Teme, high up on the bank above.

What annoyed Repton was Knight's *The Landscape: A Didactic Poem*

Opposite: Sheffield Park in East Sussex.

Payne Knight's mock Gothic castle at Downton.

published in 1794. When one thinks of Brown's nature-inspired lawn
coming up to the ha-ha one can see why Knight wrote:

> The bright acacia, and the vivid plane,
> The rich laburnum with its golden chain;
> And all the variegated flowering race,
> That deck the garden and the shrubb'ry grace,
> Should near to buildings, or to water grow,
> Where bright reflections beam with equal glow,
> And blending vivid tints with vivid light,
> The whole in brilliant harmony write:
> E'en the bright flow'ret's tints will dim appear,
> When limpid waters foam and glitter near,
> And o'er their curling crystals sparkling play
> The clear reflection of meridian day . . .

and so on, an urge to unnatural brilliance and gaiety to be compared with
the work of

> You fantastic band,
> With charts, pedometers, and rules in hand,
> Advance triumphant, and alike lay waste
> The forms of nature and the works of taste!

T'improve, adorn, and polish, they profess;
But shave the goddess, whom they come to dress . . .

Hence, hence, thou haggard fiend, however call'd,
Thin meagre genius of the bare and bald;
Thy spade and mattock here at length lay down,
And follow to the tomb thy fav'rite Brown . . .

Payne Knight did not live long at Downton but moved to London, where most of his aesthetic and antiquarian interests lay. Downton was occupied by his brother, Thomas Andrew Knight, an outstanding pioneer of scientific agriculture and horticulture, who only just missed making the discoveries in genetics that Mendel made.

Uvedale Price (1747—1829) was of Welsh origins; he received a baronetcy in 1828. Very wealthy, he travelled widely and published his first study also in 1794. It was entitled *An Essay on the Picturesque, as compared with the Sublime and the Beautiful; and on the use of studying pictures for the purpose of improving rural landscape.* It and its successors were much concerned with the views of Burke. His house at Foxley was built in 1717, surrounded by a formal garden which he landscaped in the Brown manner. This he later regretted. The views expressed in this and his other works are too complex to relate here. But it is typical of his attitude that he regretted Vanbrugh had not been more concerned with garden design. Like Knight, he praised roughness of contours and planting. And he was one of the first landscape philosophers to urge the planting of exotics in the distant parts of the garden. Unlike Knight, he was a great planter and forester. Time and subsequent developments have, however, obscured much that he did; his house is no more. But, again, we see a remarkable continuation of the ideas put into practice by Hamilton at Painshill. Indeed, in one essay, after saying that Brown and his followers had only one idea among them, he praises Hamilton for the use of his study of painting that he made at that place.

Price's essays were widely read and his influence was great, particularly among a wide circle of friends; his powers of observation still appeal to us. But that his theories were widely put into effect by a professional designer, who admittedly based his work on them, is less well known. William Sawrey Gilpin (1762—1843) was the son of Sawrey Gilpin, the successful animal painter and nephew of the Rev. William Gilpin, the student of British landscape and of the picturesque and other qualities of British trees. He himself was trained and became a highly accurate topographical artist and, though with little horticultural knowledge, later took to garden design following the picturesque principles of Price. He had very many commissions, but only recently has his actual work been studied — a good example with many original plantings being available in the arboretum at

Sheffield Park: the house in its fine setting of conifers and planting by Soames.
Opposite: Hodnet Hall is a faultless example of a twentieth-century garden.

Nuneham Courtenay, which is now an extension of Oxford University Botanic Gardens. Garden by garden his work is being traced; some of it is still in splendid condition. Further, we have his able and clearly written account of his views and methods, beautifully illustrated by his own excellent drawings, first published in 1832 with the title *Practical Hints for Landscape Gardening;* an enlarged edition was issued in 1835.

His insistence on the practice of the truly picturesque as conceived by Price is shown in his advice to a landowner who wishes to improve his own grounds: 'Consult such pictures or prints as are applicable to the case. The *Liber Veritatis* of Claude, and the *Liber Studiorum* of Turner, will afford many examples to the purpose.'

While Gilpin was working, a vast change in the planting material available totally altered and increased the whole aspect of landscaping, though, indeed, this had been increasing steadily for some years. But in 1824 young David Douglas, employed by the Horticultural Society of London (now the Royal Horticultural Society) sailed from Gravesend for the North Pacific coast of America to work his way inland to collect plants. By the time he was accidentally killed in 1833 he had collected and

sent home trees and shrubs such as Douglas fir, Sitka spruce, Monterey pine, the common mahonia, the red flowering currant, the snowberry and dozens of other trees and shrubs that thrive in and have altered the appearance of English woodlands and gardens. In 1843 Robert Fortune arrived in China and sent home more conifers, azaleas and rhododendrons, while in 1860 J. G. Veitch collected a number of plants in Japan, including the Japanese larch, now regularly a part of our woodland landscape. In 1849 William Lobb went to the ground formerly covered by

The arboretum at Westonbirt, Gloucestershire, begun by R. S. Holford in the nineteenth century, shows great imagination and vision.

The pin mill and canal terrace at Bodnant garden in Wales.

Douglas and, among else, brought back in 1853 large quantities of wellingtonia seed — a tree of singularly distinctive character that was widely planted. Then, in 1899, E. H. Wilson opened another era of plant collection which lasted until 1939 by his first visit to western China.

Within a century not only the gardens of the British Isles but much of its landscape and particularly its forests and woodlands had been altered. Two features remain visually constant, the green of the grass and the streams and sheets of water — though their manipulation and management have been made much easier, perhaps too much so.

Four good examples of the many that make full use of the vast developments and possible effects of the changes of the late nineteenth and particularly the twentieth century are Sheffield Park, Bodnant, Hodnet Hall and Wakehurst Place.

Sheffield Park in East Sussex is a National Trust property, and this body has continued to develop the garden (which stands some way from the house) after acquiring it in 1954. The main physical features are as when the place was bought in 1909 by A. G. Soames (1854-1934). There

A view in the Savill Garden, Windsor Great Park.

were already fine conifers planted, it is said, in 1800. But Soames developed the garden, making paths around the lakes most aptly designed to take many of the new trees and shrubs that were becoming known — and, incidentally, displaying the native flora to its best advantage. Repeatedly, glimpses of the lakes are seen. No comparable landscape could have been created in the days of Price and Knight, but both had anticipated its possibilities.

Bodnant in the Conway Valley is another National Trust property, vast in extent, which brings the mountains of Snowdonia within its vistas. In 1875 Henry Pochin began planting the site with rare conifers. Later, his grandson, the first Lord Aberconway (1879—1953), began planting in the wilder valleys magnolias, camellias, rhododendrons (in great numbers and variety), eucryphias and other recent arrivals sent by British plant collectors.

An even more recent garden, in the same general style but on a scale that is more human, is that at Hodnet Hall in Salop. Begun in 1921 by Brigadier Heber Percy on the site of an old garden — he himself taking an active part in its actual construction — it is a faultless example of a twentieth-century landscape of moderate size.

The countryside branch of the Royal Botanic Garden at Kew at Wakehurst Place in East Sussex, a property of the National Trust, created by Lord Wakehurst from 1903 to 1938, is a fine garden landscape.

Finally, it is right that this account of a style of garden conceived in the British Isles should end with a reference to one of the greatest and latest in this genre, the Savill Garden in Windsor Great Park. It was begun in 1932 in quite a small way but grew in size and repute. King George VI commanded that it should bear its present name after its creator, Sir Eric Savill.

NOTE

All the landscape gardens described except those which the text makes clear no longer exist are usually open to the public as announced in the press, but owing to changing circumstances this may not always be so.

I have particularly chosen as examples properties owned by the National Trust, whose opening is regularly announced.

Very few modern books have been published on the subject. There was H. F. Clark's pioneering *The English Landscape Garden* (1948). Christopher Hussey's *English Gardens and Landscapes, 1700—1750* (1967), splendidly illustrated, is limited, as the title suggests. Kenneth Woodbridge's *The Stourhead Landscape* (1971), published by the National Trust, is much more than a strict guide to that great man-made scene.

INDEX

Page   numbers   in   italic   refer   to   illustrations